A TOUCH of RHYME

by
Michael C. Eames

Published by M.C.E. Publishing

Copyright © 2008 Michael C. Eames

ISBN

This book is dedicated to the
Loving memory
of my beloved
Elsie

For tears I shed I have no shame
We shared a love that few can claim
Our parting brings both grief and pain
Yet in my heart you will remain

Contents

DREAMS

At night as I lay sleeping

There's a dream that re-occurs

I imagine once again my hand

Is holding tight to hers

I hear her gentle laughter

Once more upon the air

And my spirit wanders freely

Relieved of worldly cares

I once again revisit

Those places from the past

And recall to mind the happiness

Of moments unsurpassed

Awakened in the morning

By the cold gray light of dawn

The dream so bright and vivid

So soon is almost gone

Like pieces of a jigsaw

That lingers in the mind

No matter how you concentrate

Just never seem to bind

A whole new day before me

With many things to do

Till night again allows me

To return to dreams of you

GASTRO ENTERITIS

Now good old Paddy bought a dog to take home to
Kilkenny
He said I'll train this little pup to earn a pretty penny

I think I'll call it by the name of Gastro Enteritis
Because of what it leaves behind whenever it's excited

He kept it in a building at the bottom of his garden
So neighbours would not be upset to hear the darn
thing barking

And every day you'd see the pair together going
training
They did not seem to mind if it was sunshine snow or
raining

Around the field our Paddy ran the dog behind him
trailing
And by example tried to show it how to jump the
railings

To untrained eyes it may appear his actions were
peculiar
But he's had winners at the track to give the man his
due sir

So please refrain from rude remarks you could upset
his feelings
And after all his boyish charm's what makes him so
appealing

WINTER

When winter stalks about the land

And snow lays deep and crisp around

Although there's beauty still to see

It's by the fire that you'll find me

There's ice upon the village pond

Where Jack Frost waved his magic wand

And icicles festoon the eves

With snow a cloak for leafless trees

The winter winds cuts like a knife

And drifts of snow conceal the ice

Then on the roads you must beware

To drive with extra thought and care

The birds and beast must scrape around

To find their food on frozen ground

Some may perish, some survive

But all must fight to stay alive

For those of you who say you care

And have a little food to spare

It's now our fur or feathered friends

Would benefit from odds and ends

Those scraps of food no good to you

Could help them see the winter through

For if their plight we do ignore

One day wildlife will be no more

EGYPT

The wonder of Egypt just picture the scene

The land of the Pharaohs is just like a dream

Visit the temples and sail down the Nile

The life blood of Egypt that stretches for miles

Feluccas and dhows passing lazily by

You can easily picture the past if you try

Imagine the splendour there once must have been

When the empire of Egypt was ruling supreme

The wondrous library and medical school

The great Pharos lighthouse and mighty sphinx too

The pyramids capture the mind to this day

Why did they decide to build them this way?

So much speculation of when why and who

But who can be certain of what's really true

We think we've the answer then low and behold

We find things were not quite the way we supposed

What once thought an air shaft it now would appear

Shows the path to the heavens the Pharaohs would

steer

Those treasures of Egypt though now in decay

Once stood majestic and proud on display

Their gigantic statues alone or in rows

Neither weather nor time could completely erode

Magnificent temples will marble clad halls

And the scenes of great battles depicted on walls

The tombs where the Pharaohs were buried in state

Believing that death was but merely a gate

The start of a journey that led them afar

To as gods spend eternity up in the stars

A question that keeps coming back to my mind

Are things of importance yet still left to find

What treasures still lay there concealed by the sands

Is history buried beneath were you stand

I am sure if you visit you'll want to return

There's so much to see and so much more to learn

The magic will linger wherever you go

The spell that is Egypt will not let you go

MAN

The tropical forests that once stood so proud

Are fast disappearing should this be allowed

The beasts that they shelter will soon have no lair

Man, at destruction doe's more than his share

The natural disasters that come now and then

Can hardly compete with the ones caused by men

The future of wildlife gives cause for dismay

It will all disappear if we go on this way

When so many creatures already have gone

It's time that we noticed we're doing things wrong

If soon we don't wake up and try to atone

The only thing left will be man on his own

What for our children will be left to see?

But effects of pollution on land and at sea

Will they forgive us for what we have done?

At least if we try they may forgive some

THE YOUTH

A youth setting out on his journey through life

By a wise man was given this piece of advice

When problems beset you as surely they will

Then look for that rainbow just over the hill

The time's always darkest at just before dawn

Then follows the sun and a new day is born

Things seldom are really as bad as they seem

And tomorrow, today will be yesterdays dream

You see on life's journey there's no turning back

And the wisdom of Solomon most of us lack

So each of us must do the best that we can

To achieve the goals set in our own master plan

The youth having heeded the wise mans advice

Took comfort from this as he journeyed through life

And when in his old age he paused to look back

It was clear to him then, it had been the right track

DAWN CHORUS

To hear the dawn chorus still gives me a thrill

A pleasure indeed for which there's no bill

If I live to a hundred I'd never complain

Of the noise in the morning caused by their refrain

As age overtakes me and faculties go

That sound in the morning still gives me a glow

Everyone singing a song of its own

Each slightly different in content and tone

It seems I remember that someone once said

To be unaffected you had to be dead

MELONIE

With hair black and silky and eyes just for me

It was love at first sight when I met Melonie

She welcomed me home at the end of each day

And listened intently at what I would say

For ten years it lasted, in truth I can say

That my heart it was broken when she passed away

The deep understanding that grew through the years

Left fond memories later to soften the tears

She's still in my heart and the feelings so strong

That I often forget my Alsatian has gone

REFLECTIONS

Now I sit all alone with a memory

In a chair my the side of the hearth

And reflect on the things I once value

And of youth which for me is long past

I think now and then of occasions

When I thought I'd go out of my head

And also the friendships I treasured

But alas most of them are now dead

My body that once was so active

Seems now to be made out of lead

And when I wake up in the mornings

It's an effort to get out of bed

Now my partner no longer is with me

Fond memories are all that are left

And the house is so empty without her

But the years that we shared heaven blessed

I look back on life not in sorrow

But remember the good times I had

And whatever fate deals me tomorrow

I'll play out the hand and be glad

It's no good to spend life complaining

About how to you life was cruel

Count each day you wake as a bonus

And you won't go far wrong as a rule

THE WRITER

I sit at my computer every day when I get home

Far from interruptions, like the TV and the phone

I write a little poem or an ode or two of verse

On subjects that amuse me or on people I have cursed

It really is surprising if you pause to take the time

Just how many situations you can tell about in rhyme

In fact I would be bold enough with certainty to say

That suitable material exists in every day

Those little peccadilloes that each of us hold dear

Would make a worthy chapter if in print they did

appear

I normally compose things just to bring a smile or two

But if I am so minded there are other uses too

The pen it has been quoted is more powerful than the

sword

And wielding it in vengeance can exact a rich reward

So kindly take the warning that I hope is spelt out

clear

If you feel you must annoy me it's my pen you have to

fear

HOME

Home is a shelter from the storms of life

A place to shut out the problems of the world

Fussed over and cared for by those you love

Success or failure has no meaning here

Your presence causes the sun to rise and the birds to

sing

Any little faults you may have are tolerated

You are loved just because you are you

And if you sometimes have to queue for the bathroom

TOUGH!

SPRING

When buds appear upon the trees
And winters hardships slowly ease
We know that soon a hint of spring
Will to our gardens beauty bring

The ground is warming down below
Soon seeds will germinate and grow
The hedgerow starts to come alive
With plants determined to survive

The birds begin to build their nests
With fervent haste and new found zest
Each searches for a mate with care
So they can lay their future there

When spring comes knocking at the door
It brings a message none ignore
It's time for life to start anew
With many things to plan and do

All creatures living, large or small

Respond at once to natures call

In woody dell and leafy glade

A play unfolds on nature's stage

Soon flowers will venture into view

A myriad of vibrant hues

And as the season marches on

Till summer now it can't be long

THE DOG

Of all of the creatures god made it is true

The dog without doubt is the best in my view

When troubles beset you and friends let you down

There's one you can count on to still be around

He's loyal and faithful whatever you do

And helps to console you when you're feeling blue

For a little affection you get in return

A worthy companion as many have learned

The world may be hostile and people unkind

It's then that you value his friendship you'll find

Success or a failure in life's daily grind

To him have no meaning he just doesn't mind

Give him some exercise, food in his bowl

Remember to praise him as well as to scold

They're really like children and if treated right

Will love to be with you by day and by night

They're only an animal some people say

But is that so different from us anyway

Our specie has many traits lacking in worth

I would not presume that the dog's any worst

A GIRL IN TROUBLE

I'm only just a little girl I haven't yet reached two

And lately I've had cause to think I'll be lucky if I do

Everybody likes me that's a fact of which I'm sure

But visits to the hospital have become a frequent chore

A lunch appointment ended up with damage to my arm

And now on Karen's banister I've suffered further

harm

My forehead has three stitches now all set out in a row

What else has fate in store for me I'd rather like to

know

After all a girl must look her best when seen around

the town

And it hardly seems becoming to have stitches in your

crown

I have to trust the people who are looking after me

So please take all precautions to return me damage

free

RETURNING HOME

So many years ago it was
I left my native shore
And a longing now comes over me
To visit it once more
It seems like only yesterday
I stood beside the gate
And said goodbye to everyone
To whom I could relate

Although I travelled far and wide
There stayed inside of me
A wish that I'd return some day
Across the Irish Sea
There's a little bit of Ireland
That remained within my heart
Warmly glowing to remind me
Through the years we've been apart

I think as we grow older
We reflect on certain things
To recall to mind our childhood
For the pleasure that it brings
I'm sure despite our troubles
We can all if we look back
Find something that we cherish
Stored in our memory sack

And now that time is pressing
With whatever's left to me
I'll fulfil that long ambition
And once more in Ireland be
Though things so long remembered
Are never quite the same
I still can't stop the yearning
To return there once again

THE HOME HELP

Don't look on me with pity at my sad and lowly state

For once I had great power and caused fearless men to

quake

The wheel has turned full circle and a job I had to take

With hand brush and a dustpan I now clean out

people's grates

Now rubber gloves and apron are the tools that I must

take

As I stumble on regardless in the vacuum cleaners

wake

I accept my new position is important in its way

For old age is a condition that we all will reach one day

My only reservation is the question now of pay

A week of home care equals what I once got for a day

So I'll soldier on regardless giving comfort where I can

Till my mortgage is completed making me a happy

man

A MOUSE'S TAIL

We've taken in lodgers with four furry feet

And often hear scratching and sometimes a squeak

An increase in numbers would cause us dismay

How do we persuade them to please go away

Our cat shows no interest in hunting down mice

Preferring a pampered sedentary life

To rodent invasion it's calm and aloof

I'm sure he believes he's redundant proof

And if there's a battle defending our home

The cat seems to think we must fight it alone

So now in the evenings we sit here in fear

And wish the Pied Piper of Hamlin was here

If you've a solution we'd welcome advice

On how to get rid of these troublesome mice

THE FINAL RIDE

On each horse's head a tall black plume

And the hearse with floral wreaths festooned

The occupant lays at peace inside

Conveyed in style on his final ride

The cemetery gates that loomed ahead

Yawned open wide to receive the dead

Mourners stood by the open grave

Whilst a funeral dirge was softly played

A life had reached its allotted span

And death had now taken him by the hand

Soon earth would cover his resting place

And time his memory will erase

As the coffin sinks down out of view

Those present think of the man they knew

A grieving widow says goodbye

With a tearful gaze and a heartfelt sigh

For each of us that lives must die

Few knowing where or when or why

Death comes to both the high and low

And when he calls we all must go

None can cheat the hand of fate

Or fail to keep that final date

In life enjoy what comes your way

Who knows how long will be your stay

THE RIVER

That murmur of the river
On its journey to the sea
Like a gentle playing symphony
Of natural harmony
The ripple of the waters
Carried softly on the air
Have therapeutic qualities
That banishes worldly cares
Like a brightly coloured ribbon
That flutters on the breeze
It meanders through the landscape
Winding in and out the trees
In its bosom many creatures
Ride the eddies to and fro
Knowing only where it travels
They are also bound to go
From the mountains through the valley
It continues moving on
On its banks lush vegetation
Frame the path where it has gone
In the meadows thirsty cattle
Dip their muzzles in its flow
And the water wheel keeps turning
Grinding flour for making dough

In the light of early morning
Many creatures there you'll find
Who are visiting the river
To partake of natures wine
Where the fish are in abundance
You may sometimes have a view
Of the heron catching breakfast
Or a kingfisher or two
The river like a magnet
Attracts life of every kind
In every nook and cranny
Something lives there you will find
Water is the life blood
That transforms a barren place
An asset to be treasure
Not allowed to go to waste

THE MOON

I look up in the heavens

And I see your silver glow

Is there magic in your moonlight

I would really like to know

Are lovers blessed by moonbeams?

If they chance to walk below

Is it merely superstition

Will we ever really know

Are the sonnets just a fable

A romantic tale no more

Is it just a case of wishing

For a love that will endure

Can we ever be too certain

Of just what produced the spell

Does it really even matter

We'll enjoy it just as well

If true love it should blossom

Be it day or be it night

There's one thing to remember

Grasp it tight with all your might

THE CAT

The cat to which many have given a home

By nature was fashioned to hunt and to roam

Whilst sat by your fireside he may look demur

But don't be deceived by this bundle of fur

To all feline specie the instinct to hunt

Needs only a prompt to be brought to the front

That sweet little moggie that sits on your knee

Is a miniature lion when he's out roaming free

Like his cousin the lion by natures decree

Your cat's basic instincts quite deadly can be

Though smaller in statue he never the less

Retains all the features to kill with finesse

Another relation among the big cats

The tiger that's famed for his stealthy attack

And like his small cousin he feels quite at home

When stalking his quarry completely alone

So next time you look at your own treasured cat

As he lays there just purring stretched out on your lap

The picture you see is not all that it seems

A demon is lurking back there in its dreams

AUSTRALIA GUIDE

A wonderful country to visit it's true

A land that abounds in spectacular views

And for your enjoyment I've made up a pack

Informing you of some Australian facts

Australia harbours some creatures quite strange

With peculiar habits and odd sounding names

There's wombats, koala and platypus ducks

And a thousand more creatures that bite, sting or suck

The crocodile lurks in his billabong lair

And there's poisonous snakes you must treat with

great care

There's funnel web spiders and red backs as well

A bite from these fellows will hurt you like hell

And even the ocean where you'll love to swim

Though truly fantastic has dangers therein

There's camouflaged stone fish with poisonous barbs

And fish that have teeth in their mouths very large

These things to beware, are of various size

It's not just the big things that hold a surprise

The shark and the jellyfish visit these shores

And the small blue ringed octopus can't be ignored

The Australian tucker is really a treat

It's nice to eat out on the grass or a beach

The meat is superb and the fruit is so sweet

And the price of a meal is exceedingly cheap

The folks are quite friendly where ever you go

At least when I went there I found it was so

When they say G'Day it's like saying hello

They speak English different down under you know

Up in the mountains the air is so clear

You'd be pardoned for thinking you'd like to live here

It's such a big country with places to go

There are tropical forests and deserts and snow

The flora and fauna are often unique

And indigenous customs are full of mystique

Aboriginal artefacts aren't dear at all

You must bring a boomerang back for your wall

The didgeridoo is a musical pipe

And with practice you could learn to play it all right

In the Market Cross centre you'd draw quite a few

Playing Molly Malone on your didgeridoo

SPACE

Since the dawn of early science

Man has looked up to the stars

And wondered if there could be life

On Jupiter or Mars

So many works of fiction

That was written long ago

Spoke of travel to the planets

And one day that we would go

The fantasies of yesterday

Have changed to facts today

With technical advances

Getting better every day

If aliens are out there

From what we know it seems

They are very distant neighbours

With light years in between

The question then arises
Are they hostile or benign
If presented with the option
Would our visit they decline

For back here on our planet
When our history's exposed
Acts of violence and aggression
Is the main thing that it shows

Could it be those many sightings
Of elusive UFOs
Are an alien race accessing
Just what danger that we pose

THE BACHELOR

Love is a quandary of that there's no doubt

Did you ever just wonder what it's all about?

Can you see a grown man going down on his knees

To ask a young girl will she marry him please?

I scoff at the notion of me on my knees

That would be the sign of some mental disease

If the time should arrive that it happened I'd be

Eternally grateful if you would shoot me

I've just no intention of settling down

I prefer to be footloose, a man about town

I've seen it too often with friends I have known

Now reaping the harvest of wild oats they've sown

A wife to come home to, it sounds very swell

But she'd want to come with me out drinking as well

The barmaids I think would not fall for my charms

If I had a wife holding tight to my arm

The money I earn, I can spend as I will

With no one to nag me to pay off the bills

I'm off to the races when I have a mind

And I don't have to be home at any set time

I am my own master and that's how I'll stay

My liberty I'll not give lightly away

Of marriage there's only one thing I would say

I'd rather be happy than wed any day

THE ELEPHANT

The elephant's size makes him fearsome indeed

But his diet consists of leaves pulled from the trees

Because of his bulk it is not wise to tease

If he wished he could flatten a person with ease

Because of his strength he is quite often used

In the service of man were great weights must be

moved

A living bulldozer when he has been trained

Whose uses are many and widely proclaimed

He must be considered the very first tank

And many a conqueror had him to thank

Hannibal's conquests are well known indeed

His elephants brought Mighty Rome to her knees

His tusks made of ivory fetch quite a price

And ornaments carved from it look very nice

It may look attractive but is it quite right

When to get it an elephant forfeits its life

Although he's protected by laws in his lands

He frequently suffers from cruel poacher bands

If left unprotected it would not be long

For the last of the elephants all to be gone

So many wild creatures have suffered this fate

We must all act together before it's too late

If ivory does seem appealing to you

Remember it means that a death must ensue

To see this proud beast in its natural home

Should inspire a man surely to leave him alone

THE TRAVEL AGENT

To be a Travel Agent
You must have many skills
A knowledge of geography
And places that appeal

Be confident of manner
Be pleasant and sincere
Advise on many aspects
And allay the client's fears

Have knowledge of each country
The things you need to know
Will every day be sunny?
Or is there a chance of snow?

Your wealth of information
Should include without a doubt
Is it safe to drink the water?
Do mosquitoes lurk about?

The client should be treated

With courtesy and tact

Because if he is happy

He will bring his custom back

Remember it's his custom

That pays the wages bill

And each one that you satisfy

Puts money in the till

At times he may be difficult

He may not have a clue

But that's the time your expertise

Should make his dreams come true

His holiday is important

And you must make him feel

That you have done your utmost

To get him the best deal

A SOLDIERS TALE

I once served as a soldier
In hot and foreign lands
And my heart still feels a stirring
When I hear a marching band

The sweet smell of the orange groves
Comes back to haunt my mind
Recalling to my memory
Those half forgotten times

Those crystal clear blue waters
Where once I used to swim
And the fish in great profusion
That surrounded me therein

The snow caps on the mountains
The burning dessert sands
And the people that I met with
As I travelled through their lands

With Turks I've smoked a shisha

And with Greeks I've had much fun

But to me the Bedouin Arab

Were by far my favourite ones

For out there in the dessert

Where these rugged people roam

In their tents made out of camel skins

I was made to feel at home

Of mans material riches

They have but very few

But the little that they do have

They will freely share with you

We met it's true as strangers

From worlds set poles apart

But has friends said our good byes

When the time came to depart

The Squirrel

The squirrel in the treetop high
So agile he can almost fly
You'll see him busy gathering
The nuts to see him through to spring

A nest within a hollow tree
Provides him with a sanctuary
The squirrel's quite like you and me
He doesn't like the cold you see

And when the cold of winter bites
He hibernates there out of sight
But should he chance to wake too soon
A lack of food would mean his doom

And some will perish I'm afraid
Because their store has been mislaid
A moral here we all could learn
Put by a bit of what you earn

But when the spring at last arrives

The lucky ones who have survived

Will once again be plainly seen

Cavorting in their leafy green

The pleasure that their antics bring

To me is quite a treasured thing

In nature if you look around

There's great enjoyment to be found

COMPUTER VIRUS

My computer caught a virus and I don't know what to

do

Would anybody like to share a helpful tip or two?

I tried to write an article to send off to the press

But what comes out my printer is just anybody's guess

I understand some Arabic and some Italian too

But Double Dutch is probably the nearest in my view

I don't know how it caught it. Is the internet to blame?

Whatever is the reason it's fair driving me insane

I've tried to fix with Scan Disc and I've tried Disc

Doctor too

But neither has succeeded and I'm now in quite a stew

I've switched off and rebooted and I've even said a

prayer

Yet despite of all my efforts I still find it lurking there

Can you tell me what procedure to consider at this

time?

To eradicate this virus or at least make it benign

I'm now reaching desperation in my quest to overcome

The corruption to my programmes that this little pest

has done

I'm prepared for desperate measures to again be in

command

And will even change components if that's what the job

demands

Whatever the solution I've decided come what may

That when I give an order my computer will obey

THE LEARNER

To the ears there comes that awful sound

The crash and grind of gears

And then a cavalcade of cars

Around the bend appears

Without a doubt there'll be in front

When it comes into view

A learner with instructor

From the local driving school

A tight lipped nervous pupil

Gripping tightly to the wheel

The instructor sitting passively

With nerves of tempered steel

Although the other motorists

May shout and hoot their horns

The instructor treats their conduct

With aloof distain and scorn

For we all began has learners

And mistakes are made it's true

But one day with skilful guidance

He may be as good as you

So if it's your misfortune

To be stuck behind his car

It's your patience and forbearance

That will show how good *You* are

AUTUMN

The summer colours start to fade
As autumn sweeps across the glade
The trees begin to shed their leaves
Detecting coolness in the breeze

Though once bedecked in vibrant green
Now russet, gold and brown are seen
And all around upon the ground
A multi coloured carpet's found

The migrant birds are seen in flight
All heading south for warmth and light
And as I see them on their way
I feel regret that I must stay

The squirrel now with urgency
Seen scampering from tree to tree
Must gather up his winter stores
As near his hibernation draws

The temperature now dropping fast

To herald the first winters blast

Reminds us that before too long

Our central heating must go on

As time moves on the seasons change

Each one a scene on nature's stage

And as each season draws to close

To take its place one more unfolds

THE ACCIDENT

Have you ever noticed?

When embarrassments occur

That it's never with discretion

In the way you would prefer

I am sure that in the dessert

If you tripped over a rock

That Bedouins aplenty

Would appear to stand and mock

When carrying the shopping

Should the bag disintegrate

You can bet your bottom dollar

That a crowd will congregate

Those early morning duties

When you got up in the dark

And a keen eyed colleague spotted

You had socks one light, one dark

Like the day the ringing doorbell

Brought you rushing from the bath

And the towel caught on the door knob

And unwrapped you as you passed

Whilst you stood there in the doorway

Just as naked as you please

And the double glazing salesman

Tried to put you at your ease

And often too our bodies

Have been known to let us down

Resulting in our imitating actions of a clown

A careless step, a thoughtless turn

How easily it's done

And then before you know it

You are sitting on your bum

Then, from every nook and cranny

Comes a thousand pair of eyes

To witness your discomfort

And embarrassing surprise

THE VISITOR

I listened intently and lay very still

Every nerve in my body awake to the thrill

Could that be a reindeer I hear in the street

Or a snuffling fox in pursuit of his meat

I thought for a second that strange scraping sound

Was just like a sled pulled on uneven ground

A flurry of snow drifted down from the roof

What could have disturbed it, could it be a hoof?

A creak from the rafters I heard overhead

And my heart began pounding as I lay in bed

And deep in the chimney I swear I could hear

The rustle of movement so quiet but quite clear

And then, like a pair of boots hitting the hearth

A bump and a sound that was just like a gasp

I awoke in the morning, was it all a dream?

You know just how real at time things can seem

I went down the stairs still a little perplexed

Not sure in my mind just what to expect

I opened the door and there under the tree

Was a pile of wrapped packages waiting for me

And there in the hearth on a pile of fresh soot

Could it be a footprint or was I mistook

And so to this day it will never be clear

Was it all just a dream or had Santa been here

THE VALLEY OF DEATH

For the heights of Balaclava

Many brave men fought and died

But the charge made by the Light Brigade

Will on history's page survive

On both sides of the valley

Lethal guns had been deployed

The Brigade must run the gauntlet

With the risk they'd be destroyed

They rode into the valley

Six hundred men or more

Where soon heaps of mangled corpses

Would fill the vale with gore

A salvo from the Russian guns

Rained down on England's pride

Bringing death to horse and rider

Cut to ribbons in their stride

Yet still hell bent for glory

And to quiet those deadly guns

They continued ever onward

On that terrifying run

Lances carried at the ready

With their glinting tips of steel

Lacking military advantage

All they had was fervent zeal

Each man had just one purpose

To all dangers they were blind

They must capture Balaclava

And so break the Russian line

SHOPPING

My wife and I went out shopping

She said she could use a new Bra

The one that she had lacked in comfort

And allowed them to hang down too far

We said to a lady assistant

We would like your advice if you please

Can you tell us the size we should ask for

So they don't hang about by her knees

She said follow me for a fitting

And then said with a bit of a grin

I'm sure we've a product here somewhere

Big enough to get everything in

She took the wife off for a fitting

And returned with one after a bit

The wife said it's quite an improvement

To again have a comfortable fit

I looked at the article closely

And then with my usual wit

Said if we buy a spare one now darling

We can carry the shopping in it

And so with our shopping concluded

We drove off back home in the car

I switched on the kettle for coffee

Whilst the wife unpacked her spare bra

FREEDOM

I'll tell you a story I thinks very sad

Of what I heard said by a broth of a lad

Tomorrow said Paddy; I'm going to be wed

Says I to myself, sure I'd rather be dead

It seemed such a pity to go down that road

And carry for ever that burdensome load

To be sure she's a colleen that catches the eye

And many heads turn as she passes by

But he'll find sure I'm thinking before very long

That his freedom once cherished, alas has now gone

For a short while his life will be peaches and cream

Then a nightmare will slowly take over his dreams

I know what I'm saying I've been there myself

And soon afterwards wished I'd been left on the shelf

I courted an angel, those times they were swell

But after we married she made my life hell

It seems that my drinking was not to her taste

And a bet on the horses considered a waste

A couple of jars with the lads after work

Now how on occasions could such a thing hurt

Sure when I informed her of where I had been

Begorra you'd think I'd done something obscene

Divorce was a blessing when it came around

In the pub of a night is now where I am found

To tell you the truth what I'm missing the most

Is on Sunday, the beautiful smell of the roast

But I answer to no one, my time is my own

Has I sit with me drink in the pub all alone

Greyhound Mania

Have you heard about our Paddy

A most interesting case

He bought a pair of greyhounds

Intending them to race

He built for them a stable

At the bottom of the yard

To train them into winners

He thought should not be hard

He fed them on black pudding

And sometimes gave them white

The secrets in the feeding

You've got to do it right

The diet gives them stamina

The next thing they will need

Is a rigid training programme

For building up their speed

Patricia she could help him

Though she isn't very quick

I'll give her half a furlong start

Now that should do the trick

Patricia, such a willing wife

When asked at once agreed

To do her best to help him

In this his hour of need

So Paddy and the dogs set out

To put her to the test

Patricia wore her running shoes

And racing aertex vest

It really must have been a sight

If only you'd been there

To see Patricia emulate

The actions of the hare

A puffing panting Tricia said

What have you got me in to

Both of them have got four feet

And me I've only two

It soon became apparent

That although she did her best

He would have to find a faster hare

To put them to the test

To put them to a trainer then

It seemed was only fair

To hone their fitness to a peak

With expert knowing care

A visit to the dog track now

Is all they really need

I'm confident that on that day

I'll see them win with ease

And so another winner joined

The dog track winners club

Yes Paddy really made it

And he's off now down the pub

So if there is a moral

To this story to be told

Those four legged furry creatures

Was his route to pots of gold

Mother's Day

We meet so many people

In our lives from day to day

But there's one who's very special

That we think of on this day

It's the one who at the outset

Gave to us the gift of life

And throughout those days of childhood

Was our shield in times of strife

So to show appreciation

For those years of love and care

Make that special little effort

To enforce the bond that's there

For the gift of love and kindness

Is the best you can bestow

And Mothers Day is special

So be sure to let her know

THE NIGHT

In a world twix wake and sleeping

In the labyrinth of my mind

There are stealthy creatures creeping

From a dark mysterious time

Though forgotten in the daytime

When those shadows start to fall

That's the time when whilst I'm sleeping

Nightmare figures come to call

Though never seen too clearly

I am sure that they are there

And they're lurking close behind me

If to look I did but dare

Was it only an impression

Or did in fact I Feel

The touch of icy fingers

On my neck, it seemed so real

Along the twisting corridors

I Iwandered in my dreams

Pursued by loathsome creatures

So indescribably obscene

Like a person who is drowning

I put up a desperate fight

To evade the pit of darkness

And return in to the light

When the early rays of daylight

Start to filter through the room

Chasing out the fleeting shadows

That persisted in the gloom

Then I gaze up at the ceiling

And relief fills every pore

That another night has ended

And I live again once more

THE CAMEL

The camel's a curious creature

You may have seen one in a zoo

The dromedary only has one hump

The Bactrian camel has two

I know that some people do eat them

One said when I asked for his view

That despite the numerical difference

They both taste the same in a stew

In hot arid desert conditions

The camel comes into his own

And feeds on the sparse thorny bushes

Those other beasts leave well alone

Where water and fodder are missing

And many miles lay in between

The camel's unusual construction

Makes him quite a fantastic machine

For those who must live in those regions

And travel this desolate place

Ability counts in its favour

More than would its beauty or grace

The wandering Bedouin Arab

Gives thanks when he prays to his god

For providing a beast so adapted

And suited so well to its job

Offended he can be quite nasty

And kicks with four feet so beware

He can spit a considerable distance

So approach him with caution and care

Of charm and charisma he's lacking

A fact you will notice it's true

But I feel it is us who are lacking

If we don't give the camel his due

THE OLD FISHERMAN

An old man stood on a windswept quay

With tired old eyes he looked out to sea

White horses topped the rolling waves

And breakers crashed on the landing stage

The boats that rode at anchor heaved

And the swirling waters writhed and seethed

Pontoons creaked as they rose and fell

And men were glad they had built them well

Rigging lashed by the roaring gale

Sent forth a sad and mournful wail

And thought him glad that he should be

Safe here ashore and not at sea

The air was thick with salted spray

Yet still he felt compelled to stay

His boat no longer left the bay

But he could still recall the day

So many men had left these shores

And love ones never saw them more

The deep below became their bed

As wet as tears the widows shed

The old man gave a sigh and turned

In life one lesson he had learned

No man is master of the sea

God determines what will be

NIGHTMARES

At night when we are sleeping

Many thoughts run through our minds

Some are pleasant reminisces

Of some time we've left behind

But how many do I wonder

Dread the very thought of sleep

And those figures in the shadows

That are waiting there to leap

There's a host of evil demons

That can lurk within the mind

And although you may not see them

You are sure they're just behind

Those corridors seem endless

When you're searching for a door

To escape from that impending

Horror that's in store

Your heart is beating madly

Like a hammer in your breast

And those bands of steel are tightening

Like a vice around your chest

The ground beneath you crumbles

And you're falling through the air

You experience sheer terror

And the ultimate despair

You watch as from a distance

While each scene of fear unfolds

Is the torment to be endless

With each phobia exposed

Each person high or humble

Quite regardless of estate

Has something he's afraid of

Or some shameful quirky trait

These things come back to haunt us

When sleep unlocks the gate

And leaves us at the mercy

Of what's lurking there in wait

THE CAR

Your car will perform on snow and on ice

In ways unexpected so take my advice

Remember the distance It takes you to stop

Will now be much more so your speed you should drop

Fierce operation of throttle and brakes

Resulting in skidding are common mistakes

The thing to remember is when they're applied

A fierce application will cause you to slide

Never hurry your journey for fear you'll be late

And be extra careful when you overtake

The chances you take will all be in vain

If a place in the cemetery's all that you gain

Caution and common sense used side by side

Promotes better driving and helps you survive

CHRISTMAS TIME

The smell of cooking on the air

The table piled with Christmas fare

A feast befitting of a king

The joy that only Christmas brings

Carols on the radio

And in the sky a hint of snow

And there beneath the Christmas tree

Are packages for you and me

The glow of embers in the hearth

With memories of Christmas past

All those we wish the most to see

Can once more all together be

With glasses charged up to the brim

Lets drink a toast to all within

Long life, good luck in future years

And most of all God Bless All Here

WHO'S IN CHARGE?

I have a cat called Snowy

And one called Suttie too

In doors they are respectful

And never pee or poo

To go out to the garden

Snowy bangs the cupboard door

But Suttie's method differs

He stabs me with his claw

It's true that cats are clever

And at training they're supreme

If an owner thinks that he's in charge

He's living in a dream

They know just how to play you

And that's a simple fact

To be cute and quite endearing

He has learned the way to act

You're really like a puppet

When it comes to loose or win

No matter what you're thinking

It's the cat that pulls the strings

THE DUEL

Grey wreathes of mist on the cold still air

On the field of honour two men stood there

Their seconds carried in an ornate box

A brace of pistols with polished stocks

Each with a loaded leaden ball

And Death was waiting for one to fall

The reason for the duel was small

A chance remark at a summer ball

But neither man could now step back

Lest courage he be thought to lack

Off to one side the umpire stands

With kerchief held in an upraised hand

Twelve paces now upon command

Then turn and fire their lethal round

The duellers stood erect and calm

Portraying not a single qualm

Their linen shirts despite the cold
Were soaked in sweat so I was told
The umpire's hand dropped to his side
And each man walked with a steady stride

On reaching twelve they turned and fired
And a body fell on the reddened mire
A ball had lodged in a vital spot
And a life had come to a sudden stop

Death had recruited another soul
For a wasted life now the bell would toll
The price of honour comes quite high
When to meet the bill a man must die